Malik's First Job: Financial Tips for Teens and Young Adults

By Kerwyn S. Phillip, MBA

MALIK'S FIRST JOB

Publishing Consultant:
The Pierce Agency, LLC, USA
www.ThePierceAgencyLLC.com
804.549.2884

Cover Design Courtesy of Natasha Payne-Brunson (IG @artsylibrarian)

Printed in the U.S.A.
ISBN -13: 9798581530108

For reprint permission, or to use text or graphics from this publication, e-mail your request to
Khufu.enterprises.llc@gmail.com.

Table of Contents

Acknowledgements

First, giving thanks to The Most High, and all my Ancestors who paved the way for my existence. My parents, Randolph and Venita Phillip, and my siblings, Melissa, Allan and Kira. I wish to thank my wife, Aniysa, and my children, the three that walk with me: Menkuara, Khefera and Kush. And the one that watches over all of us, Khufu Nehisi Ankh Re.

The Brothas on Da Ave, The Jersey City Crew, Morgan State University, Xavier High School. A special thank you to: Dr. Franklin Caesar, Kym Grinnage, Natasha Payne-Brunson, Dr. Shantell Chambliss, Rebekah Pierce, Stephon "Coach" Hicks, Angela Patton, Ray Patton, Bro. Kindu, DJ Sayeed, Roderick "Chip-Fu" Roachford, Jonathan "Jaz-O" Burks, Michelle Burks-Hogan, Vinson "Wordsworth Johnson, Taiwo Odunsi, Kehinde Odunsi, Sean Young, CJ Walker, Marc Lamont Hill, David Miller, St. Christopher "Zeb" Robertson, Brian Holloway, Uncle Bunn, A.J.Varmah, Diemiruaye Deniran, Meldon Jenkins-Jones, Patty Parks, Pamela Jones, Kelli Lemon, and Clovia Lawrence.

Dedication

For Aniysa, Menkuara, Khufu, Khefera, Kush, and all
future generations.

Malik's First Job: Financial Tips for Teens and Young Adults

Malik Prepares for His Job Interview

Today's the big day. Malik is getting ready for his first job interview at Mr. Solomon's Sneaker World on Pitkin Avenue. Pitkin Avenue is located in Brownsville, Brooklyn. For a 3-mile stretch, the streets are lined with a wide variety of stores and street vendors. People can purchase clothing, shoes, beauty products, art, electronics, and a host of other items. Mr. Solomon's Sneaker World has been located on Pitkin Avenue for over 25 years.

Malik is really excited because this is an opportunity for him to land his first job and the environment would be perfect for him because he's really into sneakers and fashion. As he gets ready for his interview, he puts on a pair of khaki pants, a white dress shirt, and a navy-blue blazer that his father helped him pick out. He wants to stand out in the interview, so he throws on a red bow tie. He chose the bow tie, instead of a straight tie, because he feels it would add a little flare to his outfit. Now, the white pocket square and light brown wingtip shoes that match the color of his belt. The brother is ready to land a job!!!

"Mom!! Dad!! Wish me luck. I'm on my way to my interview at Mr. Solomon's."

"Good luck, son. If you interview as well as you look, you will definitely land the job."

Malik heads down to Mr. Solomon's Sneaker Store. Mr. Solomon has seen all the latest trends and styles that have come and gone. In the 80's, young people were into shell-toe Adidas and suede Pumas with the matching tracksuits. During the 90's, it was baggy jeans with FUBU, Phat Farm, or Karl Kani. Most recently, the fashion trend has become more colorful and less baggy.

Mr. Solomon likes to hire young people from the neighborhood. This gives him the opportunity to mentor and teach them life skills that they will need in the future. Even though Mr. Solomon already knows who he is going to hire before the interview, he puts his applicants through a formal hiring process so that they understand how to communicate and present themselves in professional situations.

As Malik walks towards the sneaker store, he passes his friends, Damion, Stretch, and Kyle, who are hanging out on the block.

"Looking sharp there, homeboy!! Coming through looking like a million bucks," says Damion.

"Peace, fam! What's good?" asks Kyle.

The guys laugh and give Malik a pound. "Peace, what's good?" Damion replies.

"Peace, I have an interview with Mr. Solomon at his sneaker store."

Stretch exclaims, "That's what's up!! Mr. Solomon is a good dude. He really looks out for the community. He gave my brother, Will, a job back in the day, and taught him a lot. Good luck, Chief!!"

"I appreciate it. I'll holla at y'all later."

The Job Interview

Malik continues to Mr. Solomon's store. As he's walking, he thinks about the questions he believes Mr. Solomon will ask him and how he plans to respond to them. After about 15 minutes, Malik arrives at Mr. Solomon's store. He's a bit nervous because although he has visualized the interview, he still doesn't know what to expect.

One of the workers goes to the back room where Mr. Solomon's office is located to let him know that Malik has arrived. Mr. Solomon is a tall, intimidating-looking man. He stands over 6 feet tall and has a muscular build. He looks like he can play middle linebacker for the Pittsburgh Steelers.

He appears from the back office and greets Malik with a firm handshake. "Peace, good afternoon, young man." He then invites Malik into his office. As they are walking to the back, Mr. Solomon states: "First, let me say that I love how you dressed for the interview. The way you dress gives people their first impression about you. If you saw a person in a police uniform, you would think they were a police officer. If you saw someone with a helmet and shoulder pads on, you would think they were a football player. In the same way, when you see a person dressed in a shirt, tie, and jacket, it's safe to say that the person is about business. The fact that you came dressed professionally lets me know that you are serious about getting the job. Thank you."

Upon entering the office, Mr. Solomon tells him to have a seat. Malik has shopped in the store for several years but has never been to the back of the store before, nor Mr. Solomon's office. He scans the room for objects that can give him a clue about Mr. Solomon's personality and interests. This was an interviewing tip that his dad shared with him. It will help to gather talking points to engage Mr. Solomon to learn more about what his interests are outside of work.

Malik looks around and spies a family portrait on Mr. Solomon's desk. *Ok, he has a wife and children, maybe grandchildren*, he says to himself. There are also autographed pictures of Brownsville-natives Mike Tyson, Riddick Bowe, and Zab Judah standing in front of the store. A framed Patrick Ewing poster adorns the wall (*He's a boxing and NY Knicks fan*), and there are various books on his bookshelf. Malik scans some of the titles: *They Came Before Columbus*, *The Isis Papers*, *The Autobiography of Malcolm X*, *Think & Grow Rich: A Black Choice*. "He's a reader," Malik says under his breath.

"Okay, Malik, let's begin. Tell me about yourself."

"Well, Mr. Solomon, I'm a Senior at Boys & Girls High School. I'm an Honor Roll student who plays football and I'm also part of the chess club. I enjoy playing video games, hanging out with my friends, and listening to music."

"What position do you play on the football team?"

"I play defensive end."

"That's a fun position. I used to play defensive tackle when I was in high school. What is the biggest life lesson that you learned from playing football?"

"Playing four years of football has taught me a lot about planning and goal setting. But I think the most important lesson it has taught me is how to bounce back after failure. There are times when you may miss a play or two in a game. After those downs are over, you have to forget about those plays and focus on the new downs to make something happen for your team. So, the same thing happens in real life. You can't worry about what happened yesterday. Every day is a new opportunity to make an impact in the world around you."

Mr. Solomon was impressed. "Wow! Great insight. That's a very important lesson. So, what are your plans after high school?"

"After high school, I'll be attending Morgan State University in Baltimore, Maryland. They offered me a full academic scholarship."

"Congratulations!! That's wonderful! I know it's a great feeling to have your college tuition already taken care of. Have you decided on a major?"

"No, sir, not yet. I'm torn between Political Science, Business, and Mass Communications. The only thing that I'm sure of is that I want to use my degree to help my community here in Brownsville."

Again, Mr. Solomon found himself deeply impressed and liking this young man even more by the second. "That's very noble of you. It's important for us to give back. So, tell me, why do you want to work for me?"

This was it! The moment Malik had prepared for. He took a deep breath, visualized the outcome he wanted, and began: "Like most kids around here, I'm into clothes and sneakers, so I would be very comfortable working here. Plus, I get to interact with people and help them with their purchases. In addition, Mr. Solomon, you are a highly respected person here in Brownsville. I feel that I can learn a lot from you, especially with me wanting to come back after I finish school."

"Thanks for saying that. I appreciate it. I've lived here for quite some time and have seen people come and go. It's important to plant yourself somewhere, build roots, and plant seeds. When I say plant seeds, I mean to find ways to spread your positive influence to those around you and uplift others in your community. Community is extremely important. When you analyze the word 'Community', it can be broken down into 'Common Unity'. Find those living around you and find a way to work together for a single goal. I offer opportunities to young people who want to learn and better themselves. Now, let me ask you, why should I hire you?"

Malik took another breath: "I would be an asset to your store. I am hardworking and I have a good knowledge of the latest fashion and sneaker trends. Also, I get along well with others and have great customer service skills."

"You mentioned the latest fashion trends. When you look at yourself, do you consider yourself a leader or a follower?"

Malik puts his hand on his chin and takes a moment to think about how he wants to answer the question. "When I view myself, I think I'm both."

Mr. Solomon is taken aback at Malik's answer. "Both? I never heard anyone say that before. Please explain what you mean."

"I've come to realize that in life there are times when you have to take the lead and other moments when you have to fall back and follow someone else who may have more knowledge than you. I think it's part of the balance found in nature."

"Hmmm. interesting … Do you have any questions for me?"

"What is the biggest challenge that you are dealing with in the store?"

Mr. Solomon thought for a moment. "I think the biggest challenge we face here is trying to manage our inventory, along with keeping up with the latest trends and styles. The hottest styles seem to change more rapidly now than they did in the past. So, when ordering items, we have to order just enough to sell and not be left with excess inventory that we can't get rid of when that particular style changes. Managing that can be difficult at times. That's a great question. Anything else?"

"No, sir. I don't have any more questions," replies Malik calmly. He was inwardly sitting tall. He was proud of himself.

"Malik, I am very impressed with you. At this time, I would like to extend the job offer to you. You can start next Monday."

Malik was excited. He shook Mr. Solomon's hand, said thank you, and took off home.

After running for over a mile, Malik comes crashing through the front door, screaming excitedly, "Mom!! Dad!! Mom!! Dad!!"

Malik's parents, Kedar and Anosha, along with Malik's siblings, run out of the kitchen in a panic. "What's wrong, Malik? What happened?" asks his mother, Anosha.

Malik responds, "I got the job! I got the job!"

"Congratulations, son!" exclaims Kedar.

"That's great, baby!" says Anosha as she hugs Malik.

Manny reaches out to give his brother a pound and yells, "That's what's up!!"

Nubi and Nefertari gave Malik a congratulatory hug. "When do you start?" his father asks.

"Next Monday," replies Malik.

"Wow!! My son has joined the working class."

"What will you be doing?" Anosha asks.

"My brother got a job with Mr. Solomon!! Now I can get all the latest sneakers," blurts Nubi. The family all laughs.

Malik answers, "Mom, I'll be working as a Sales Associate. My job will be to help customers, maintain the sales floor, and unload trucks when new merchandise arrives."

The following day, Malik meets his friends outside to share the great news, "Peace, y'all! What's going on?"

Damion, Kyle and Stretch all say, almost in unison, "Just chilling."

Malik then goes on to say, "Guess what? I got the job with Mr. Solomon."

"That's dope!! Congratulations!" says Kyle.

Damion follows. "Yeah, man, congrats!!"

"Great news!" says Stretch. "When do you start?"

"Next Monday."

Stretch continues: "Now Malik will be stepping through with all the latest drip. We definitely will be stopping through to shop with you."

"No doubt, appreciate it," says Malik.

"Now that you are going to be making some consistent bread, you got to be careful not to spend it all in one spot," says Damion.

"What you mean?" Malik asks.

Damion responds, "I've seen too many cats who work complain that they never have money. I don't understand how you can work, get paid, then say you have no loot. I don't know how other cats get down, but I make sure I keep bread in my pocket."

"I hear that," says Kyle

Damion continues, "Years ago, my Uncle Maurice put me on to game and showed me how to properly manage the money that I get from work. Malik, you should chop it up with your pops to see if he can school you on a few things."

Malik Seeks Financial Advice from His Father

Now that Malik has the job, he wants to make sure that he manages his money correctly. People he knew that worked always complained that they didn't have any money. How can you have a regular job and never have money? To get a good handle on his finances, he asks his father for guidance.

Kedar says, "Son, now that you have a job, I think it's time for you to learn the basic principles on how to manage your money. These concepts were taught to me by my father when I was a teenager and got my first job. My dad, your grandfather, wanted to make sure that I had a good understanding on how to manage money because he saw many of his friends mismanage money and struggle to make ends meet. When he and your grandmother first got married, they struggled for a long time. He eventually figured things out and was able to establish and maintain financial stability. The lessons he learned, he taught me, and now I'm going to teach them to you.

These concepts, if applied, will put you ahead of your peers and serve you well into adulthood. Most people lack the knowledge and discipline needed to properly manage their money. Go get a pen and notebook so you can write down these principles, and refer to them as needed."

Malik goes to his room, grabs his notebook and pen, and then returns to the dining room table to listen to his father.

Being Rich vs. Being Wealthy

Malik's father begins. "So, to begin, do you know the difference between being rich and being wealthy?"

Malik is confused. "Dad, isn't that the same thing?"

Kedar responds, "No, son. They are not the same thing. They are totally different. The main difference between being rich and being wealthy is knowledge. Wealthy people know how to make money, while rich people only have money. For example, if you were to win the lottery and come into a large amount of money, then you would be considered rich. But once you lose that money, you would not know how to get the money back.

On the other hand, if you were to establish wealth, then you would have had to work hard to build your wealth over time. It would take a process, and once you mastered the process, then you would know the steps to create wealth. That's why you see many multi-millionaires who may file bankruptcy take a fall but then end up re-establishing their wealth over a period of time. They understand that there is a formula that requires focus and discipline, and always works when applied.

The problem with most people is that they have little patience and want immediate gratification. There is no such thing as a get rich quick scheme. Many lottery winners often win large amounts of money and then within a few years, they lose it. Similar things happen to athletes. They get drafted and earn huge multimillion-dollar contracts, but since no one has sat them down to teach them the difference between assets and liabilities, they end up going broke within a few years after retirement. Do you know the difference between an asset and a liability?"

"No, sir."

"Ok, we'll discuss that in a little bit." Kedar continues: "To start off, at the top of the page, I want you to write the title, "9 Keys to Building Abundance." Okay, so let's begin. Write the numbers 1 through 9 down the left margin of your paper. Now, the "9 Keys to Abundance and Wealth" are:

1. **Create a Source of Income**
2. **Pay Yourself First**
3. **Discipline Your Spending**

4. **Invest a Portion of Your Savings**
5. **Seek Wisdom from Professional Experts**
6. **Play Your Position When it Comes to Assets and Liabilities**
7. **Create Multiple Sources of Income**
8. **Avoid Debt Like the Plague**
9. **Be Grateful for What You Have and Be Charitable**

"You got it?"

Malik smiles: "Yes, sir."

"Great! Now, let's talk about each one in detail."

Chapter 1 ~ Create a Source of Income

"This is where you start on your pursuit to building abundance. In order to start on your path to obtaining wealth, you must have a source of income. This source of income can be from various sources. Some people start a business, work at a job, sell things online, provide a service, etc. Sometimes, you have to think outside of the box. In some cases, you have to identify a problem and develop a solution to that problem. Most people are willing to pay to make their problems go away. For example, the average adult may realize that their car is dirty or that their grass needs to be cut. With the hectic schedules people have today, one may not have the time, or are perhaps too tired to handle these tasks. As a result, they will hire someone to take care of these tasks.

If a young person is eager, they can find plenty of opportunities to create income. In this case, both parties benefit from the exchange. The person who is paying to have these jobs done is happy to get the tasks done and help teach a young person responsibility at the same time. The teen provides a service and gets paid to do so.

Having a formal job, and working for an employer, is not the only way to generate a source of income, however. Here are some ideas for generating income:

- Clean houses

- Babysit or Pet sit

- Wash cars

- Cut grass

- Shovel snow

- Sweep at barbershop/beauty salon

- Sell products online (flea market)

- Create/Sell t-shirts online

- Social media marketing

- Tutor kids

- Collect cans/bottles

There are probably more ways that I missed, but this is a good start. Take some time and do some research.

There's a great book that you should check out called, *Rich Dad, Poor Dad,* by Robert Kiyosaki. In the book, the author explains that there are four different ways to earn income. First, you can earn income as an employee. That is when you work for someone else and are paid a salary. Secondly, you can be self-employed. A self-employed person does not have a job, but they own a job. In this case, people like barbers, lawyers, auto mechanics, and doctors can be considered self-employed people. The only drawback to being self-employed is that if you don't work, then you don't get paid. For example, if you are a barber and you can't work because of an illness, then you can't earn money while you are out.

Next, is the business owner. This person owns a business and gets paid whether or not they are at the business. In the same example as before, if the barber owns the barbershop and has other barbers pay booth rent, then if he is out sick, he will still collect booth rent from the other barbers.

Another example would be a restaurant owner. The restaurant owner does not have to be present for the day-to-day operations of the business, but they still earn an income. If you had an issue with your order, you would more than likely take your issue to the manager because the owner probably won't be there."

Finally, he speaks about the investor. "An investor is a person who puts his or her money into a business endeavor in hopes of earning a profit. When you watch television shows like "Shark Tank", the "Sharks" are investors seeking out opportunities to help struggling businesses by giving them money in exchange for part ownership in the business. The part ownership they purchase is also called equity. By purchasing this equity, the investor has an opportunity to share in the business' profits in the event the business does well. The next point is crucial to establishing wealth."

Chapter 2 ~ Pay Yourself First

"This is the foundation to building and maintaining wealth. There is a common mistake that is made by most people. They go to work with the mindset that their only objective is to go to work to earn money so that they can pay bills. In your case, you want to work so that you can buy the latest video game system, or the hottest pair of kicks. Once they receive their paychecks, people list all the financial obligations that they have. They pay the light bill, car payment, phone bill, groceries, etc. But they often forget the number one financial obligation, which is themselves. When you bring money home, it is critical that you pay yourself first. You are the number one reason that you are working. Take at least 10% of what you earn and pay it to yourself.

Now, that doesn't mean that you take that 10% and go spend it on worthless things. That 10% is money that you put away, save, and don't touch. You allow that money to build and accumulate. Over a period of time, you will have built a financial reserve that you can use for emergencies, investments, and other obligations that often spring up from time-to-time. That way, when these surprises arise, they won't impact the money you have budgeted for other bills. With you saving 10%, you are training yourself to live off the remaining 90% of your income.

Let me write it out on paper, so that it makes more sense. Let's say, for example, that your gross income, which is the money you make before taxes and other deductions are made, is $450. After taxes and other deductions are made, your net income is $400. Now, 10% of $400 is $40, which is the amount that you will pay to yourself. The remaining $360 is the money that you will live off of. After 10 pay periods, if you continued to pay yourself $40 each time, you will then have $400 in savings while still living off the remaining $360 each pay period. Now, if you are able to raise that percentage to 15-20%, then you would allow yourself to build a larger savings. At this point, you'll be living off 80-85% of your income.

Paying yourself first and sticking to it helps to build your financial discipline. While you are in the process of putting this money to the side, you will be tempted to spend it. All types of "unbelievable deals" will come across your table. The key will be to set your priorities (yourself) and stick to them no matter what. Once you see the cash reserve grow, and know how hard you worked to build it, you will find it easier to stick to your plan. As in most things, it will be most difficult when you first start. But overall, it's a great financial strategy. Once you have the money put to the side, I'll explain what to do with it in a few."

Chapter 3 ~ Discipline Your Spending

"Once you have been able to position yourself to save a portion of the income that you bring home, it won't mean a thing if you haven't disciplined your spending. As you work to build your cash reserve, all types of non-important wants will arise. Oh, the electronic store has a new Super-Mega-Ultimate Triple High-Definition Television on sale for an unbelievable price! Yeah, go ahead and spend the money that you took time to save! What's going to happen when you have to pay for major repairs to your house or vehicle? You have to maintain a long-term vision that will keep you focused on the objectives that you are trying to reach. Is it going to be easy? No. If it was easy, then more people would not be in a bad financial state."

Find Motivation

"To help establish this discipline, you must establish what your "why" is? Why are you saving this money? What is your long-term goal? What are you trying to accomplish with paying yourself first? Your answers to these questions will help you create the motivation that you'll need to stay focused on your savings goal. For example, you may be saving to purchase a car that you can use to get back and forth to work, or maybe you want to build up your savings so that you have cash available for a rainy day. Establishing the "why" will give you a focal point when the distractions arise.

Let's say you're working and saving up to purchase a car. Your friend stops by and asks if you want to go to Miami and hang out for the weekend. You've saved the money and can afford to go on the trip, but you would need to use the money you saved for the car. So, now you have to stop and think about what is more important: the car or a few days in Miami."

Create SMART Financial Goals

"One method that is very effective in helping people create meaningful goals is the SMART method. The SMART strategy is a plan that people use to develop and set their goals. SMART is an acronym that stands for Specific, Measurable, Achievable, Relevant, and Time-based. This strategy can be implemented in any goal that you are trying to achieve.

SMART Goals				
Specific	Measurable	Achievable	Realistic	Time-Based

Let's use an example of you having a goal to save money.

The first letter is "S," which stands for "Specific." This means that the goal has to be clear and well-defined. So, your goal is to save money, but you haven't established how much you want to save. Next, you have to make it "Measurable," that's the "M." So, to make this goal measurable, you have to add a dollar amount. It can be $1,000.

So far, your goal is to save money and the amount is $1,000. Is that "Achievable"? Yes, it's achievable because you have a job, and you have the means to save money. OK, that's the "A" in SMART. Next, is "Realistic," the "R." Saving $1,000 is achievable and realistic. If you were to say that your goal is to save $1 million, is that realistic based on your current salary? No, it's not.

Finally, you have to set a deadline and set a time limit, or else you'll be trying to achieve this goal forever. What's the time deadline? The end of the summer? Ok, so your goal is to save $1,000 by the end of the summer by putting away 10% of your income per pay period. This is both achievable and realistic."

Create a Budget to Track Your Spending

"It is important to track your spending and creating a budget will make it easier for you to do so. By writing down the money you earn and what you spend it on, this helps you to become more conscious of your spending habits, which will then lead to becoming more disciplined. Quite often, you will hear people say that they got paid on a particular day, then a few days later, they complain that they have no money and have no idea what they spent it on. They did not keep track of how they spent their money. It is important to monitor spending habits and create a budget. A budget helps you to create a spending plan. As it is said, if you fail to plan, then you are planning to fail, and far too often when it comes to finances, a lot of people fail.

A budget is an estimate of your income and how you plan on using it to pay bills. Most budgets are set for a certain time period. A budget is important because it's a written plan on how you intend on allocating your income. It's best to have a written plan because it helps you to evaluate your expenses. It also protects you from those unnecessary spending moments. If the expense is not written down, then it may not be that important. However, there will be instances where unexpected emergencies arise. Your written budget will allow you to analyze your expenses and make adjustments to accommodate those financial emergencies."

	Jan.	Feb.	March	Total
Income				
Salary	$800	$800	$800	**$2400**
Gifts	$50	$0	$0	**$50**
Other	$0	$100	$0	**$100**
Total Income	**$850**	**$900**	**$800**	**$2,550**
Expenses				
Pay Self First (10%)	$80	$80	$50	**$210**
Food	$250	$200	$100	**$550**
Clothing	$175	$200	$200	**$575**
Transportation	$75	$100	$100	**$275**
Entertainment	$89	$50	$100	**$239**
Video Games	$150	$50	$150	**$350**
Other	$0	$100	$0	**$100**
Total Expenses	**$819**	**$780**	**$700**	**$2299**
Gain / (Loss)	**$31**	**$120**	**$100**	**$251**

Evaluate and Re-Evaluate

"As you continue to grow and manage your money, it is important to take time, every so-often to evaluate where you are financially. The only thing that is constant in the universe is change. As time goes on, you will experience changes in your life, and you will have to adapt to those changes. For example, after working at the sneaker store for about a year, Mr. Solomon might be impressed with your work ethic and want to offer you a raise in your salary.

Let's speak hypothetically. Let's say that you receive a raise and now you get an extra $30 per week in your paycheck. How are you going to factor that extra $30? Are you going to put the full amount into your savings? Maybe you will use it for extra spending money for when you hang out with your friends. You might want to split it in half and save $15 and add $15 to your hanging out money.

Another example is if you receive a pay cut. Let's say you end up changing jobs and the new position that you have pays you $30 less per week than what you were making at the sneaker store. In this situation, you will also have to make adjustments to your budget. You will have to account for the $30 reduction in income and reduce your spending. Are you going to save less money by reducing how much you save, or perhaps hang out less with your friends, or spend less on clothing? Either way, these examples will have a direct impact on your income and cause you to make a few changes to your budget.

Even beyond the potential pay increases and pay cuts, as you mature, your personality changes, which makes your wants, desires, and needs change. There are things that as a teenager you view as being important now that in a few years you will no longer feel are as important. Right now, having the newest sneakers and fresh gear is vital, but in a few years, your focus may be different, and you may want to spend your money differently."

Malik interjects. "Hold on, dad. I will forever be fresh!!!"

"Haha! You say that now, but as you mature, and take on more responsibilities and have to make serious decisions on how to spend your money, and then you may feel differently. Right now, you have a cushion because you live with me and your mother. But when you move out on your own, have your own bills, and have to choose between those retro Jordan's and a light bill, then you may feel differently."

"Well, with what you are teaching me, I can budget and keep a stash for my kicks, and I'll be good. That way I can be fly and still keep the lights on."

Kedar grins proudly. "Ok, I hear you, brother."

Chapter 4 ~ Invest a Portion Your Savings

"After you put a portion of your income away in savings, it would be wise to take a portion of it and put it in a place where it can multiply. There are different options that you can use to accomplish this goal. A good rule to keep in mind is what's called the "Banker's Rule" or "The Rule of 72." It's a rule used to calculate simple interest. If you know the rule, understand it and use it to your advantage, then it can help you stay ahead of the game when managing your finances. Remember, everything that I'm teaching you today, I want you to take some time and research on your own."

The Rule of 72

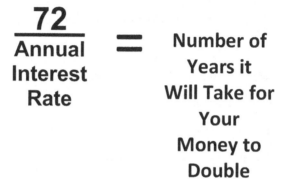

$$\frac{72}{\text{Annual Interest Rate}} = \text{Number of Years it Will Take for Your Money to Double}$$

$$\frac{72}{9}$$
(9% interest rate)

8
Years for your money to double

"Basically, when studying the Banker's Rule, you will realize that the higher your interest rate, the faster your money will multiply. Some people just take their savings and place it in a bank savings account. Saving money is good, but you have to be wise in knowing where to place the savings. The average savings account earns less than 1% interest annually. The average rate of inflation is 3%. Inflation is the general increase in prices from year to year. If prices are rising by 3% each year, and your money is only growing at 1% rate, then you are losing. The point is to put yourself in a winning position.

Some products that you may want to consider are stocks, mutual funds, business investments, and real estate. Some of these options you may not be old enough to purchase on your own, but we can look into opening a custodial account. A custodial account is a financial account that is set up for a minor and is managed by a responsible person known as a legal guardian or custodian. In this sense, I can open the account with you, help you manage it, and then transfer ownership to you once you turn 18 years old."

3-6 Months of Living Expenses in Reserve

"As you get older and grow into adulthood, it is good practice to have 3 to 6 months of living expenses saved in a reserve account. This is kept just in case there is an emergency, or some other unforeseen circumstance where you may lose your source of income. If that happens, you have money saved that you can fall back on that will help you manage expenses until you replace the loss of income and get back on your feet."

Savings Buckets

"When saving your money, it is also a good practice to separate that savings into three different categories, or "buckets." The first bucket is for long-term savings, the second for short-term savings, and the third is for an emergency fund. These three buckets will serve different purposes in your life. Let me explain:

The first bucket, which is for your long-term savings, is normally saved for your retirement. This is money that you are saving that you are not going to touch for a long time. Once you reach the point in your life where you no longer want to work, you will still need to have a source of income. If you plan ahead, and start saving early, you can position yourself to be financially comfortable when you are older.

There are different ways to save for the long-term such as: Certificate of Deposit (CDs), Stocks, Mutual Funds, and 401(k) plans.

Certificate of Deposit (CD) – a financial product available at banks that allow you to save a certain amount of money for a fixed amount of time at a fixed interest rate.

Stocks – a financial product that allows you to purchase part ownership of a corporation.

Mutual Funds – a professionally managed investment fund that pools money from many investors to purchase financial assets.

401(k) – a retirement plan that allows employees of a company to save and invest money that is put aside for their retirement without paying taxes on the money until later. Normally, when you use one of the long-term investment options, there can be a financial penalty for taking the money out early.

The second bucket is for short-term savings, which will be used toward short-term financial goals, such as buying a house or a car, or some other higher priced item that you're trying to purchase. With short-term savings, you want to make it a bit easier to have access to the money for when it's needed. In this case, you can put your money in a regular savings account, or a short-term Certificate of Deposit account.

Finally, your third bucket is an emergency fund, which is separate from the other savings accounts. The emergency fund will serve in the event of unforeseen circumstances such as house repairs, medical bills, and car repairs, or anything else that may come up that is an emergency. This money should be kept in a separate savings account from the others."

Chapter 5 ~ Seek Wisdom from Professional Experts

"When it comes to money and finance, it's a good idea to work with a financial adviser who can provide you with professional financial advice. Some people will tell you that a financial adviser is not needed, but I disagree. A doctor is an individual who went to school to study medicine and provides guidance to people on their physical, and sometimes, mental health. Similarly, a mechanic provides guidance on how to keep your car running efficiently and repairs cars when they are not operating correctly.

Financial advisors have invested time to learn how money works and provide guidance to people on strategies to better meet their financial goals. You provide them with your current financial status and what goals you want to achieve. They will then take the information that you provide and develop a plan for you to follow to help you reach the goals that you set for yourself.

Your mother and I work with a friend of mine named Winston Foster, who is our financial advisor. Several years ago, we sat down and let him know what our goals were. He helped us set up our retirement accounts, savings and investments, and our life insurance. If you like, I can have him help you out as well. When it comes to financial planning, it is never too early to get that plan in place. Actually, it is best to start early because then you have more time to build your accounts."

Chapter 6 ~ Know the Difference Between Assets & Liabilities

"An asset is something that puts money in your pocket or accumulates value, while a liability is something that you purchase, and it loses value as time goes on. You see people spend money on flashy clothes and expensive gadgets. These things are nice to have, but you must understand that those purchases can put you in a financial hole. For example, let us say you paid about $500 for some Jays and you started wearing them. Once you put them on your feet and start rockin' 'em, they can get dirty and scuffed, and the sneakers are no longer worth the $500 that you paid for them.

Now, think about if you took that same $500 and invested the money in an account that earned 5% annual interest for 5 years. In 5 years, that $500 becomes $638. If you wear those sneakers for 5 years, they will be dogged out, and probably won't be worth anything.

Investing $500 for 5 Years at a 5% Annual Interest Rate					
Original Amount (Principle)	1 Year Later	2 Years Later	3 Years Later	4 Years Later	5 Years Later
$500	$525	$551	$579	$608	$638

Another example that I can tell you about is when you purchase a car. A car automatically loses value right after you buy it. If you purchase a new car from a dealer, as soon as you finish the paperwork and drive the car off the parking lot, it is no longer considered "new"; it is now a used car. Experts say that the car loses about 10-15% in value after you buy it.

Let's say you bought a brand-new car for $15,000. As soon as you leave the dealership, the car is now worth about $13,000. So, if you drove around the block and wanted to sell it back, you would have lost $2,000. A worse situation is if you had to get a loan to finance the car. A bank will loan you the money to buy the car and you pay the bank back. Depending on the interest rate the bank charges and the term they set up the loan for, you can possibly pay 2 to 3 times the amount the car is worth. Also, keep in mind the value of the car goes down as time progresses; that is called "depreciation." This is why I advise you to save your money and purchase a dependable used car that can get you from Point A to Point B.

Don't compare your situation to someone else's. Everyone's situation is different. A lot of young people admire celebrity lifestyles and try to mimic that lifestyle when they really can't afford to. There is nothing wrong with having a role model that can help you develop a lifestyle that you one day want to have, but you must understand that you have to be focused, disciplined, and responsible to reach that goal. Just because you see your favorite rapper wearing $500 sneakers, it does not mean that you can afford to do the same thing with a minimum wage salary. I've seen too many people go broke trying to impress others by spending money on things that they really cannot afford."

Chapter 7 ~ Create Multiple Income Sources

"You currently have a job, so you have a source of income. That's not to say that you can't find other sources of income. It is best to have multiple sources of income. This is important, especially as you get older, because it's like sitting on a chair with one leg. It's pretty hard to balance on that one chair leg. If you have four legs, then you are stable. The less legs the chair has, the less stable the chair is. Now, if you are balancing on one leg and you lose that one leg, then you will end up on the floor. If the chair with four legs breaks one leg, then there are three other legs holding up the chair. The same thing is true with an income. If you lose that one source of income, then you don't have anything to fall back on. If you have four sources of income and lose one, then you have three others that will support you. If you lose two, then you still have two others."

Building Multiple Income Sources

"It is also critical to have more than one stream of income. Most adults only rely on the income they receive from their full-time job, not realizing that at any given time, they may get fired, the job may close, or any other situation can occur where they are no longer employed by that one particular company. Once that income is gone, they have nothing else to fall back on.

Think about the chair analogy again: if a chair has six legs, and you remove one of those legs, the chair will still be stable. If you remove two legs, this chair will still stand. So, it's in the same sense; if you have more than more than one source of income, you have something to fall back on. In other words, even if you lose one source of income (a leg from the chair), you can rely on that second source to hold you down until you replenish the missing source (leg). But, let's say you have three or four sources of income. Then, if you lose that one, you will still be OK.

Other benefits to having multiple sources of income are that it protects you from the dangers of unemployment; it helps you to build wealth faster if you have more income coming in. The 10% that you put to the side will be much larger and you can build that reserve source much quicker. Also, it helps you to save money faster, which will impact your ability to build wealth.

Job   Cutting Grass

Selling Items Online   Creating Websites

Here are some examples of multiple income sources. You can earn an income from your rental properties, in addition to your full-time job. You may also own stocks that you earn dividends on, or you may invest in businesses that get a return on investment. You may sell stuff online through an online business and be able to earn what is called residual income. This is income you earn while not physically working.

Some people feel comfortable having more than one job, for example, having a full-time job and a part-time job. There is nothing wrong with having more than one job, but you are limited with the number of hours you can work. You put yourself in a better position by creating income streams that work on their own. Working hourly, you only have a limited amount of time within a given week, and your body can only do but so much work before it gets tired."

Chapter 8 ~ Avoid Debt Like the Plague

"The only reason people fall into debt is when they have to borrow money because they don't have enough money to cover their expenses; if you apply the concepts I'm teaching you now, then you will have no need to fall into debt and to borrow money. The problem with borrowing money is that the borrower becomes a slave to the lender, meaning that you are spending money before you earn it, and when you get the money, it's automatically goes to someone else and you're not able to utilize it yourself. Therefore, it will be harder for you to save the money that you're now spending - the money are supposed to be saving.

The money you are earning should be going towards your bills and other expenditures. You do not want to increase your debt by paying back loans and other debts that you borrowed from other people; also, what often happens is when you borrow money, you have to pay it back with interest, which is a fee that is charged for you borrowing that money.

So, let's say, for example, you want to buy a television and it costs $1,000, but you don't have the cash to pay for it, so you use a credit card to pay for it. When you use the credit card, it's like getting a loan from a bank that you must pay back. Since it's a loan, you will then have to pay interest for the loan. Also, the amount of interest you pay depends on the rate that the credit card charges.

Depending on how long it takes you to pay back the money on the card, you may end up paying $1200-$2000 for the television that originally cost $1000. So, you end up paying the extra $200-$1000 for an item which you didn't have to, and most of the time, this is done for items we do not necessarily need but items that we want. Sadly, we're not willing to wait to pay for things. Here's the lesson: you may say that if you see something you want, go ahead and put money to the side and save (delayed gratification) in order to pay things off with cash. But the problem with humans is that we do not want. We hate delayed gratification. In addition to being able to get rid of the debt and not worry about it, you achieve a certain peace of mind knowing that you do not owe anyone any money.

In regard to credit and financing, if you don't make payments on time, it can impact your credit score."

Malik's eyebrows raise in thought. "Dad, what is a credit score?"

"Alright, let me explain what credit is and how it works. There are two terms that you will hear from time to time: one is debit and the other is credit. Debit is money that you spend from your own personal bank account. Credit is money that is lent to you from a bank. The money accessed from your bank account is from a debit card, while a credit card is used to spend the money that is loaned to you from the bank. Every time you use your credit card, you are borrowing money from the bank, which has to be paid back with interest.

The history of your money borrowing habits is kept on a credit report. This report lets other people who are thinking about lending you money know how good you are at paying money back. The report has a record of all the credit accounts you opened and the record on your payments. Did you pay on time? Were you late with your payments? How many people do you owe money to? There are 3 different credit reporting agencies, and they are Transunion, Equifax, and Experian.

Based on your history, you are then given a credit score. A credit score, or FICO score, can range from 300 to 850, and this number summarizes your credit history. Just like your report card has grades, the score you have tells the reader how good you are at paying money. The better you are at managing your credit accounts, the higher your credit score. The higher your score, the lower the interest rate you will have to pay when you borrow money.

For example, I'm going to speak hypothetically. You want to borrow money to purchase a car. When you go to the dealership, they make you fill out an application. They gather your employment information and housing information. They may even ask about your other financial obligations. Once you complete the application, they will use your social security to check your credit. When they check your credit, they see that you have a score of 700. With that score, they may lend you the money and say that your interest rate is 5%.

Now, let's say they check your credit, and the score is 600; they may then offer you the money at an interest rate of 15%. The reason for that is because with a lower score, they feel that you are a higher risk, and they may have more difficulty collecting the money from you. These reporting agencies determine your overall score by analyzing your payment history, how often you use credit, length of your credit history, how often you try to open new credit accounts, and the type of credit accounts that you open.

Nowadays, many companies check your credit for different purposes. For example, some companies run credit checks on potential new employees. They feel that the way you manage your credit reflects how responsible you are."

Chapter 9 ~ Be Grateful for What you Have and Be Charitable

"Once you have built up your savings, you must be appreciative for what you have. There are many people who are struggling and have not learned how to utilize their skills, talents, and resources to build a sustainable income. Don't ever look down on anyone. At any given time, a streak of misfortune can take everything away and you can find yourself as the person begging on the street corner. Also, if someone asks you for some money, if you have the money to spare, and you feel comfortable helping them, then do it. Never judge someone who is down on their luck. We all need help every now and then.

Sometimes, the universe puts us in a situation to test our nature. Are you a giver or a taker? Are you willing to help your fellow human being? It's not always about giving money; it can be a situation where you are being asked to give of your time. We should seek to treat others how we want to be treated because what goes around comes around.

There are many charities and non-profit organizations where you can make donations. These organizations are normally charitable in nature and often need financial support from the community to keep their doors open."

Conclusion

"OK, Malik. Remember these principles that I taught you. They will help you become a more financially aware adult as long as you practice them. Also, take time to research these principles and see how you can apply them to your life. Do you have any questions?

"I just want to make sure that I have these written down correctly. I'll summarize the 9 back to you," Malik responds. "First, I have to find a way to create a source of income. Once I have a source of income and start earning money, then I have to pay myself first before I pay anyone else. The money that I have after paying myself first, I have to manage it by having discipline as I spend it, and not go crazy with it. Part of me being responsible as I manage my money is to save some of my money and not spend it all. You also said that it is wise for me to seek advice from someone who I trust that is knowledgeable on how to manage money.

As far as assets and liabilities, assets are things that increase in value and can make more money, while liabilities are things that decrease in value over time. It's important to spend money on assets if I am looking to build wealth. Having one source of income is very risky. If I were to lose that one source of income, then I will be in trouble financially. I should seek multiple income streams just in case I lose one. Then, I have a second or third to fall back on. Next, do not develop the habit of borrowing money, and avoid being in debt. Accumulating debt is spending money before you earn it. If you have to pay someone else, then that takes away from you paying yourself. Finally, show gratitude and be charitable. What goes around comes around. If you help others in need, then the universe returns the favor, and you will see good things happen in your own life."

Malik puts down his pen and exhales. "Thanks, Dad, for taking the time to teach me these principles. I can't wait to get my first paycheck so that I can start putting these into practice. I'm going to need your help in putting my budget together. Also, dad, can you help me open a bank account when I get my first check?"

"Of course, son! We can definitely do that."

AUTHOR BIO

Kerwyn Phillip, MBA is a Brooklyn, New York native who earned his undergraduate degree in Accounting from Morgan State University and his Master's in Business Administration from Averett University. He is the Founder/CEO of KHUFU Enterprises, LLC, an organization that teaches leadership, entrepreneurship, and financial literacy to youth in under-served communities. He is also President of the Youth Business Exchange (www.y-be.org), which is a non-profit organization that promotes and supports youth entrepreneurship.

In addition, Mr. Phillip is a Hip Hop Historian. He shares his passion for the genre through his "Hip Hop Youth Empowerment Workshops." The purpose of these workshops is to highlight the impact that young people have had on the birth and growth of the billion-dollar Hip Hop music industry. Mr. Phillip currently resides in Central Virginia with his family. To learn more about his programs, visit www.khufuenterprisesllc.com, or @khufullc on IG/FB/Twitter.

Made in United States
Orlando, FL
09 August 2023